SWEET TEMPTATION

Volume I

She Sizzles

Nissi Sing

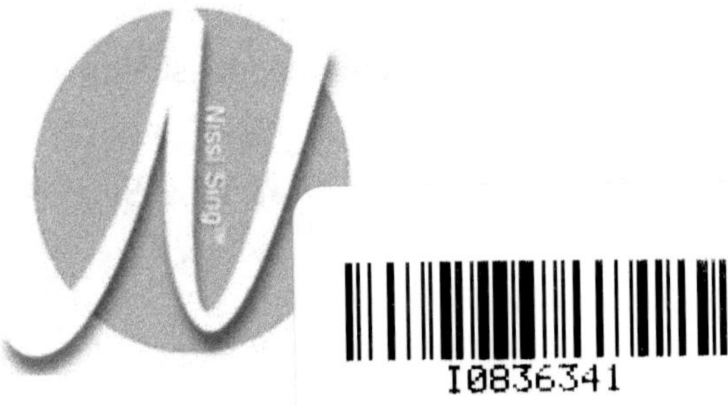

Sweet Temptation
Volume I
She Sizzles
Copyright 2020
Nissi Sing

Editing by: LaVerne Montgomery

Cover by: Elite Photo Club

Contact Information for Nissi Sing:

Instagram: @nissi_sing
YouTube: Nissi Sing
Facebook: Nissi Sing
Tik Tok: nissi_sing
Snap Chat: Nissi Sing

DEDICATION

This book is dedicated to the Sweet Temptation: A fire that fiercely flamed, a sweet desire so passionate and sensual, with deep emotions so powerful as to escape physical damnation; a Transformation of love. Formed expressions that are sure to get underneath the skin and cause the heart to skip a beat. Sweet Temptation; untainted love that draws you close and unintentionally, yet so innocently, reaches deep down into the forbidden parts!

PROLOGUE

Sweet Temptation

A sweet temptation
Is a temptation you feel deep within
Passionately, emotionally, sensually

A sweet temptation
Is a memory of
What you wish you
Could of, would of, should of
Done

A sweet temptation
Is a memory of
What you wish you
Could of, would of, should of
Explored

A sweet temptation
Is a memory, a sweet memory of
What you wish you
Could of, would of, should of
Not ignored

A sweet temptation
Does not leave you bored

A sweet temptation
Doesn't end in physical damnation
With desires touched
And untamed lusts
Pain, disappointment and
Broken relationships filled with deceit

Oh no, you see, a sweet temptation
Is when you are weak
But the God within you
Is stronger than what meets the lust of the eyes.

TABLE OF CONTENTS

TABLE OF CONTENTS cont.

TABLE OF CONTENTS cont.

She Sizzles

Phases of You

Last night before I slept
I envisioned you caressing me real good, in
Various ways, day after day
Okay, maybe I was just horny
Then this morning
I lay in my bed for two and a half
Extra hours unable or really
Refusing to get up and go to the bathroom
Mesmerized in thoughts of you
Coming to a conclusion that
You love me and refused to let me go
I visualized various ways of you
Finding your way to propose to me
And claiming me to be your very own
Am I caught up in a fairytale alone?

Years ago, I'd dream a little dream
And with the pass of the week
The dream would fade away as
Would my fantasized desire
But not this time, not with you
It's been well over a year
And here I am, still
Dreaming of you, reminiscing, missing
Everything about you, my soul yearning.

It seems you fit the description
Of the Handsome Prince in the
Fairytale that lies within me
You see, for years I was with a
Man, who promised me that
The fairytale within me could never

Become my reality and so mentally
I had decided to just give up this hope
But you came along showing off your character.
Then my heart began to send shouts to my mind
And as I looked deeper into you,
Your character makes my heart glow
My soul sings sweet melodies
My body romantically sizzles hot and
My mind, my mind records thoughts of you
That play, rewind, and fast-forward
Over and over again.

I wish this was just an expression of a
Poet exaggerating her love
Before an audience just to receive an applause
But it's not, instead
It's an unexaggerated true story of a
Woman sending a message of love to
The One she so deeply loves.

Am I somehow causing the One I love
Emotional chaos because my affection for
Him is too deep for thought?
Am I taking too literal
His creative expressions of love
Written from his thoughts of me?
Is it possible for this love to
Become our reality, or
Will we foolishly leave it on paper in
Romantic expressions of poetry?
Will we allow fear to overpower our
Passion to capture and cultivate a
Love that our souls await?

Do we have the courage to
Dare to ever-so boldly step into this
Higher realm of faith
Unleashing profound emotions of
Mysterious love
Forbidden by the world around us?

I promise you
I really wanted to write a message
Relieving you from having to think of me,
My emotions, or my perplexing feelings for you
I wanted to write so that just maybe
You could forget about me and go on with life
Instead, I'm so helplessly writing the truth
I am in love with you and
I want you, your character, your body
In my world, my space, in my life
Under the covers, between the sheets
Face to face, you and me
I want you in every way possible
And in ways unheard of just yet
They say the emotion of love is blind and
I'm starting to think it's true
Because whatever your imperfections are
I'm terribly missing them when I see you
Maybe I'm blinded by the sparkle in your eyes
When you stare at me
If only for just one moment,
You could see what I see when I stare at you
Then you would no doubt understand
Why I feel the way I do
I love you… I do….

Fighting Temptation

When you said good-bye, I never thought
You'd be gone for long
But today I believe nothing went wrong
Instead, everything went just right
Joining together can be scary, yes this is true
Except when it's *True Love*, it has the ability
To free one's thoughts and abide in pure humility
Thus, leaving behind doubt and fear.
True Love opens the eyes of the heart
And hears the heart of the mind
Which causes one to tell no lies.
Sometimes I wonder, you've wondered
Are we meant to be?
Our hearts say yes, our minds say no, or
Is it really our circumstances that tell us so?
Sweetie, I do not believe in coincidences
But every single incident has its purpose
Its meaning
Your smile, brightens my day in so many ways
And the thought of your touch
Electrifies my body so much
And your voice, hmm, your voice
It's got me falling for sure!
If you took it *there,* Would I dare to stop you?
Well now, that depends on where "*there*" is
Because please believe, I have no need
Of a sexual fling, and I'm very-well pleased
That you encouraged me to confide in you
About anything, and I'm honored
That from your heart
You believe that you would never hurt me.
Well, as you read throughout these expressions

You will see, I'm confidently confiding in you
Pouring out my heart humbly
I'm serious too, no kidding.
Baby, if I let my inhibitions go
Then a moment just won't do, no not with you
So, do you think you
Want to stand to test our energy, Do you?
I have no desire to tease me, or you
But I'll do all I can to keep us both
Safe from unnecessary pain.
And as for turning these tables,
You have the power to do so, but I advise you
First, search yourself
Make sure what you feel is true
And I admit, I need to do the same.
I also agree, Fighting Temptation is a mutha
And it's definitely way too hot in here
But before we take off all my clothes
I wanna know everything about you
No one else knows!

I ain't trying to give you 50 for 50
And 99 isn't enough
If we do join together, I promise 100 percent
100% Love, 100% Honesty, 100% you and me
Oh yes, I'm coming/Cumming correctly!
I'm tickled that you think that it would
Take just one simple kiss
Because if you look a little deeper
You'll see, I'm already in a schoolgirl bliss!
Now journey with me back in time for a moment
The night of the wedding
I assure you, the word "No"
Escaped my vocabulary, and I really believe

It was about to go down that night
Don't think either one of us was able to
Fight Temptation; do you remember?
Our chemistry was sooooo strong,
But as God is our witness
His way of escape stopped us from going so wrong
Again, I don't believe in coincidence
And I know what I feel isn't just by chance!
Now, when all *this* hits the fan
And we know that it will
We can express to the world
The "True Meaning" of Fighting Temptation
We can honestly say:
"Nothing happened back then
We fought a good fight
And though we had mad opportunity
And it was extremely tempting
Physically, we did what was right
We considered loyalty, honor, & respect
We never failed to neglect
The *Heart* of our matter
We kept in mind, that if we took it *there*
Hearts would only shatter
However, today here we stand
And from our souls, we love so deep
That our hearts won't let us sleep....
So to our Readers, Audience, and Listeners
Say what you want
Have your own opinion
But as for "Us"
We, are no longer, Fighting Temptation
Because *Holy Matrimony* is now
What we are facing!"

The Very Moment

The very moment our eyes met
I nearly lost control of my balance
Because the connection was so strong
That from my head to my feet, I felt it
I didn't know what had hit me
Never thought it could be Cupid
But very quickly my mind got my body together
And so, slowly I moved towards the window
Rapidly collecting my thoughts, I said a prayer
But that prayer went unheard
Because you moved towards the same window
Dang.
Then your eyes began to speak to my Spirit
Awakening my Soul—No, No
Where was the one I had grown to love
Over the years, I needed to be rescued
Yes, my love appeared and as we shifted gears
In a moment of relief, I exhaled
Thinking I was safe, but in minutes later
There we were again, face to face
And as I sit here today, I think back to
The very moment our eyes made contact to
The short, simple letters that said "Hey You" to
The day I heard your voice over the phone to
All the sweet, little ways you catered to me
In my home, to the night you left to
The night of the play to, the day at the library to
My knowledge of your decision to believe in Jesus
To the day I knew you were back in prison to
The night I read your first response to
Here and now to
The very moment our eyes made contact

And now, I get it
It was at that very moment
You captured my soul and ever since that moment I
haven't been able to let you go
I carry you in my Spirit, in the depths of my Soul
And though none of this was intended
My unhappy, yet very comfortable days are ended
So, could you be my Happily Ever After
My Today, my Tomorrow, my Forever
My Knight and Shining Amor.

Fallen

Could it be that you have fallen for me?
Could it be that I too have fallen for you?
Could it be that we have both fallen seriously, intimately?
We have been lost in each other, verbally
Enjoyed each other's company
Our eyes have met on several occasions
I bet our thoughts have intertwined too
Our smiles, perhaps, have left us with a clue
And yet, are we still clueless
Could it be that we have fallen mutually?
I mean maybe, you are really feeling me
As I am feeling you, but yet
I have no clue and neither do you
Circumstances tell us that this is bizarre
But memory serves me with flashbacks
Of this becoming reality
Intimate dreams of you and me untold
Forbidden desires about to unfold
Right before our very eyes
Disguised in harmless chit chat
Could it be a fact that both of us
Have fallen, increasingly?
But nevertheless, amuse me
Are there sincere desires to
Make a true friend in me
Honestly, what do you see in our future reality
Have you indeed fallen for me?
Could you think for a moment that I
Have fallen for you
Now what must we do, me and you
If it is in fact true
That we have both fallen!

What Do I Call You?

My heart calls you Friend
I truly do adore you
Yes, it's true
Though it's quite difficult to understand
I didn't choose you
Our encounter was not planned
There were no intentions for us to connect
But somehow, you've captured a piece of me
So, what do I call you?

My dreams call you Lover
Sexual desire does exist
Contemplations of a simple, sweet kiss
Passionate feelings for you grew
Overnight it seems
Continual thoughts of you and me
Together, conversing, showering
Oh my, what do I call you?

My mind calls you Bitter-Sweet
Because every thought I think
Is sensationally sweet
Yet, bitter to the core
Like no other has ever been
You are oh, so significant
As I apply self-control
I try to let go
But your essence pierces my soul
What should I call you?

My body calls you Temp-ta-tion
A sexy romance waiting to happen

Yet, I did not fall for you intentionally
And there is no proposal
For you to have me sexually
This is a complicated, yet provoking situation
But it can really be nothing more
Than a sweet, sincere dedication
To you, from me
Endurance is the key
Nevertheless, in the meantime
What do I call you?
Or better yet
What do you call me!

Tell Me

Tell me something
Do you remember me
No, I mean do you
Remember
Do you reminisce
About the late nights
The moments
Looking into each other's eyes
Being lost in conversation

Tell me,
Do you recall
The innocent, yet tempting
Occasions
Have you forgotten
Those minutes, hours
Nights, all nights

Tell me
Am I somewhere
In the back of your mind
Or am I not there at all
Was I the only one
To have taken this fall

Tell me
In your own words
Please, do sum up this situation
I would not dare ask you
To break any "Bro" codes
But tell me
Do I mean "*something*" to you, too!

Let Us Overcome

We've already crossed the line
We have entered into the deep
But still, let us delay physical gratifications
And our heads up above the water to keep

If we sink now
We will surely drown
In a whirlpool of lustful desires
And passionate anticipations

We must remain afloat
Remember the significance of loyalty
Let us not defeat
The essence of respect

We mustn't neglect
The heart of our matter
Just because we're in the deep
Doesn't mean our affections should shatter

Instead
We must endure this battle
Find our way
Back to the shallow

And as the waves continue to flow
We must hold our breath, say a prayer
And rise above the moments
Let us overcome this temptation

Let us overcome!

Tell Me Something

When you look at me
What do you see?
Are you thinking of how you want to do me?
Hold my legs up and enter me
When you talk to me
What is ever on your mind
Is it how you want to make love to me
Or perhaps just stroke me from behind?

Tell me something
When you think of me
How do you feel?
Don't you dare lie
Tell the truth
Tell me
What do I "do" for you?

Tell me something
What is it you expect from me?
I mean, I can't neglect my responsibility
Although I do have interest in you
But tell me
What do you really want to do,
What do you really want from me?
Speak your piece, state your claim
I'm just wondering what you hope to gain?

My Needs

Will you handle my every need???
And Baby trust my guarantee
Nothing in the stores will do for me
I don't need no diamonds, gold or jewelry
No house, no car, nor material luxury
What I need comes from the inside
That part of you that you hide
The part of you that rejects and dismisses pride
That place where all negativity died
I need that bond that keeps our souls intertwined

Won't you give me pure honesty
Every ounce of your integrity
The real you, for the real me
Faithfulness for an entire eternity
Let "US" forever Be

Baby, I need all of you
Priority over your friends and your crew
Over your money and associates just to name a few
I need your trust, your commitment and loyalty too
I need you to keep me forever singing, I Do.

Sweet Temptation

A sweet temptation
Is a temptation you feel deep within
Passionately, emotionally, sensually
A sweet temptation
Is a memory of
What you wish you
Could of, would of, should of
Done
A sweet temptation
Is a memory of
What you wish you
Could of, would of, should of
Explored
A sweet temptation
Is a memory, a sweet memory of
What you wish you
Could of, would of, should of
Not ignored
A sweet temptation
Does not leave you bored
It doesn't end in a physical affair
With desires touched
And untamed lusts
Pain, disappointment and
Broken relationships filled with deceit
No, a sweet temptation
Is when you are weak
But the God within you
Is strong.

Temporary Crushes

Hmmn, he looks good
Kind of hood
But a nice guy within
He wants to be my friend
He has captured my attention
And did I mention he's caused me to blush.

Dang, I got a crush on him
He constantly looks at me with a smile
All awhile we are flirting with our eyes
Mesmerized in conversation
Untamed flirtations
Imaginations working overtime
Passionate thoughts
Running through our minds.

But this is just a crush
So, look but do not touch
Soon it will be over
And I'll stop desiring him
And he'll let me be
But we will always secretly
Remember back when
We were temporarily crushing.

Attraction

Some attraction we have here
You look into my eyes with a glare
We share a quick stare
Then, your thoughts wonder where?

I wonder what you are thinking
Wishing or hoping for
What is it that you imagine?
Knowing we can do nothing more than talk.

Mentally, emotionally attracted
Desires never to touch
Is this real, or just a simple distraction
Do we seriously have an attraction?

Just Look at Me

Take a look into my eyes
Now stare a little deeper
Tell me what you see my dear
Tell me what you dreaming
Just look deep, and you will see
That I am in to you too, and if you blush
Then I will know that you are feeling me SO.

Unbelievable

You have deeply touched my emotions
Your words have caused me to smile

You've looked into my eyes
And captured my attention for a long while

It's quite amazing how we've
Conversed for hours night after night

You have surely befriended me
Yet, we've managed to do what's right

It is unbelievable how close we've bonded
In such a short time

And God only knows
What thoughts have paraded
Through our minds

We are unbelievable.

Energy

I know this can't be real
But somehow, I can feel
A sense of strong energy
When you are close to me
I know you feel it too
But still, this can't be true
We're like totally opposites
When we're near
It's like a positive and a negative
Attracting into energy.

I know this can't be real
But every time you look at me
I feel energy from your eyes
Glaring into mine, staring deep inside
Slowly, passionately, intimately
And when I look at you, I know you feel me too.

We've never really touched
I think we're afraid to
The energy may be too powerful
Electrifying our minds, emotions, and hearts
Taking us in too deep, down to the forbidden parts.

How Do You Feel?

When I come around
What thoughts go through your mind
When you look at me
Do you get a twinkle in your eye?
Have you stared at me for a hot moment
And felt a rise in your nature

Have you stared into space
With the thought of me and you
Have you imagined that
You and I could embrace for a moment or two
After falling sound asleep
Have you found me in your dreams
How do you feel
And for me, do you care?

Have you created room for me in your heart?
Have you went out of your way
To make small talk with me
When you speak to me, what do you feel
Do you often wish
Your imagination would turn real
Tell me
How do you feel?

I'm asking because I'm curious
Do you want a piece of me?
Do you ever wonder how I feel?
Would you like to touch me, rub me
Taste and see; okay, I'll stop there
Because in reality I know you care
But, we mustn't take it there.

Are You…

Thinking hard
Wishing something would give
Dreaming in your sleep
Feeling deep emotions
Hoping for the best
Are you searching for answers?

Are You…

Contemplating on taking action
Praying this all works out
Focusing on passionate ideas
Digging into your heart
Staring into space
Are you falling for me?

Wishing

I wish to know
How many times
Have you looked at me
Passionately
How many times have you
Wanted to place your lips on me

I wish I really knew
How many times in a day I cross your mind

I wish I knew
How many dreams I am a part of
How many songs remind you of me

I'm wishing for answers
Knowledge with understanding
Will I ever know
Won't you tell me so

I'm wishing and wishing
Because it's you I've been missing.

You Don't Know

I bet you don't know
That I'm missing you so
That I really do care
And my feelings for you have grown.

I bet you don't know
How you've touched my heart
How you're on my mind
And I was attracted to you at the start.

I bet you don't know
You creep into my dreams
You make me smile
And I really liked hearing you Sing.

I bet you don't know
I got it bad for you
I wish I could talk to you
And I like the way you say my name; I do.

I bet you have no idea
But neither do I
So we should keep it that way
And we'll commit no crimes and tell no lies!

Bizarre

I think it quite bizarre
That I can't seem to stop
Thinking about you
And I don't know the reason
Why I'm missing you like I do.

This is the most bizarre thing
I tell you
Because it makes no sense at all
But you've somehow
Captured a place in my heart.

It's strange, peculiar; totally bizarre
I don't belong to you
And you don't belong to me
But no matter how silly
I'm missing you
Really.

Ironically bizarre
I tell you the truth
In some crazy way
I think
I may have fallen for you
How bizarre is that!

Confused/Not

In so many ways I want you
But I really don't

Thoughts of you sexing me
But then that sounds crazy

I picture you walking into that door
Grabbing me and fiercely kissing me
Who am I kidding?

It's really not you
But the time that we shared
The conversations so friendly
The late, late nights
Yet, so innocently
I simply miss what you gave me
And wouldn't you know
It's truly amazing!

When the Sh** Hits the Fan

The truth has already hit the fan
And it took me awhile to get here
But the love I desire and seek
Is from God, not man
I must admit
It was quite foolish of me
To think that I
Had found this love
In another guy
And you said it just right
At the same time, I choose
I lose
And yes, you are still significant
But no, not the recipient
Because I do not have your whole heart
And the truth is
No,
I could never handle that!

"Optimistically Speaking"

Optimistically speaking,
God has a funny sense of humor
Because the minute I think
I got it all figured out
I'm so wrong
And when I feel desperately hopeless
I'm strong
And though what we feel
Never made any sense
I accept the truth
At my heart's expense
"Optimistically speaking,"
God is getting my full attention
Because what I was so eagerly willing
To give to you, is all He ever wanted
So optimistically speaking
I'm back to where I started
It's time for me to just
Trust my creator, my maker
Whole-Hearted!

Choose Faith

Fear of the unknown
Is the downfall of many men
What if I choose wrong, he worries?
Well, may I propose
What if you choose faith?

Scary, I know
Because with faith, anything goes
But faith in God is always the best way
Because even when you're low and it really hurts
There's no way to go, but up
Choosing what you know because it's comfortable
Is weak, don't you think?

Stop focusing on everybody's circumstances and
Looking for some type of proof
Search your heart and soul
There's really only one you truly want
If there were no circumstances, absolutely none
Which would you choose?
Then, choose her or else in the end
You, my friend, will lose.

And don't worry about fate because
In reality, fate is inevitable—it's fate
What will be, will be
And yes, only time will tell
The best part about that is
Time can heal all wounds.

In essence, the truth is what I sought
And that is what you gave

Though it left me with a broken heart
I respect you even more
Because the truth is always worth knowing
Jesus also told us it would make us free
Considering that, I love you even more
Because the truth you gave, freed me.

And right now, in your time of need
A sincere friend you truly have in me
And there is no loss to either one of us
Because you can never lose what was never yours
I tossed you my heart and
Respectfully
you gave it back to me
I greatly appreciate that and
I thank God for you, your truth
And may we both achieve a lovely new start
In faith!

It's A Wonder

All we really have is
What I now consider
A possible eighth wonder to life
And that's feelings that run deep
With no understanding of why….

Why did we meet, why do we love
Why didn't we physically cheat
Why now, why this way
Why not totally let go
Why the confusion, why such deep admiration
Why the passion to write about it
Why not just forget about it
Why does it hurt, why does it feel so real
Why are these feelings mutual
Why?

Why is the sky blue, why is the night black
Why do the seasons change, why does it rain
Why do oceans run so deep
Why the mountain's peak, why do clouds move
Why is the Earth round, or is it really flat?

And that right there leaves us with the simple fact
We just really don't know—why
And a union of you and I
Would merely be the world's eighth wonder to life
And though, at times, I wished
I had the pleasure to be your wife
It's now a wonder
How I'm going to whole-heartedly
Let go of that solitary wish!

Dear Self

Look at you
You walk with your head held high
Portraying to be so strong
Seeking to encourage everyone
But now look at you
You need the encouraging words now
Right now, you feel very, very stupid
But you're not
Maybe a bit naïve and foolish
Take responsibility for your mistakes
You did open one door without closing the other
So now you're crying over two brothers
For one of them, take no blame
He abused you, you suffered his pain
But let's look on the bright side
And let's analyze your mistake

You're suffering from a heartbreak that
You didn't have to experience
You could've left well enough alone, but you didn't
So, cry until you can't cry no more
Then stop seeking to fall in love with a man
And simply seek love from your creator
Remember this pain you feel, don't you forget it
Brighter days will come but enjoy your time alone
Be happy with yourself
You can make it on your own
Now move on and be that
Strong woman you portray!

"Pessimistically Speaking"

I feel real stupid right now
I've been dissed by a man
Whom I never even kissed
And I tried to give my heart to someone
Who was not even available
And the irony of that
Is neither was I
Now all I can do is cry.

How could I fall in love with
Someone whom I've never intimately hugged?
Crazy….

How could I take such a huge risk
And be so wrong all in one?
Dumb….

How can I appreciate a man telling me
He loves me, when he really didn't?
Naïve….

Everything I wrote before this
Was me being as strong and courageous as I could
Now this is me being hurt, because I am
Reality.

Finally

You are a bright young man
And you're probably saying damn
How did I break her heart?
But listen to me and hear me good
Take no blame because I misunderstood
You were just being you
And I was totally impressed
When you wrote your first response
You were clearly speaking the
Thoughts of your heart and I have no doubt that
You truly do admire me and you thought
A couple of times that you would love to
Have me, love me, hold me
But the fact appears
You never believed that you would
And so, you swept me off my feet
Never knowing that you could
Ironically, in the midst of everything
You apparently found love
Never again underestimate
The power of your words
And in my heart, you're still all that and then some
So, if it doesn't work out with her and you fall back
Let me be the one to catch you
Finally, what you got to say about that….

Do You Really Want to Know?

You left a bright young man with your wife
Night after night
A man you thought less of, but you weren't right
You encouraged her to mentor him
Through his problems
I bet you never imagined that she could solve any

Now do you really want to know what happened?
She watched him and she listened
And she looked inside him and saw greatness
She respectfully closed her mind to this
And began to blindly encourage him.

Intending to uplift his spirit
She ministered Jesus to him and
Her belief in the scriptures
But she didn't know that the whole time
He was really listening to her.

And so, as the time passed, and the nights moved on
They began to talk for hours and hours
Without really knowing and
Before she could realize what they were doing
It was too late; she had already noticed.

The outside of him, gorgeous from head to toe
Again, she respectfully fought her lustful desires
Crying out to her Heavenly Father for strength
Not to act on these feelings and
Believe it or not, they successfully made it through

By the grace of God, they would birth
The Sweetest Temptation ever known to man
No touch, no kiss, no sexual fling
No physical anything

Sweet Temptation they would compose of
Their intriguingly enticing experience
So, if you ever really want to know
This is the gist of how they did it.

Hope

I will always be grateful to you
You gave me hope, if nothing else
Hope and confidence that
I can experience true love

That I can really love again, whole-heartedly
You made it easier for me to gain the assurance
That another can truly love me, unconditionally

For that, I love you
From the bottom of my heart
I thank you for this hope and so
In faith, confidence and hope
I move forward in life
That I may experience true love
Abundantly, magically with another someday
Even if it's not with you!

Imagine This

Hours have I spent with you in mind
Thoughts of you holding me
Kissing me, caressing me
Taking a hold of my body
But my true desire intimate and pure
Sweet and deep, dream with me:

We're at your place
You make sure we're alone
I'm lying in your bed
Awaiting you to join me
You are showering.

As you get done
You peek out at me
To make sure I'm okay
While showing me how good
You look in a bath towel.

But nevertheless
You get dressed
And make your way to bed
Then we talk and we talk
You talk me to sleep, literally.

I awake in the midst
To see you gazing at me
Sharing precious moments of your history
Then very gently
You fall fast asleep.

We sleep the night away
And in the sweet morning
I awake to breakfast
And a beverage you've made
Especially for me.

We totally enjoy each other's company
Then seal the afternoon
With an endearing kiss
From my forehead to my upper-left cheek bone
And down to my cheek.

Then our lips meet
We hug as if we never want to let go
Again, your lips touch mine
And we humbly
Say good-bye or maybe hasta luego.

Hooked

You indicated that we were caught up
But let me express we must be hooked
Despite the relationship, still, you got me shook
And Baby, I just don't get it

Somehow, you've touched my emotions
In a unique way
Day after day, got me wishing
You would call just to say, Hello
Can't let this flesh get the best of us
Consumed with lust, dreams of you holding me
Innocent small talk, yeah right
Our conversations lasted all night

But this is a road we mustn't travel
Just unravel our thoughts in sweet poetry
And after the storm, the sun will shine
Because in reality, I ain't yours and you ain't mine
But man, we must be hooked.

A Heavenly Life in Heaven

Just one night, huh?
Let's get this understood
If one night feels good
Then rest assured
You'll want one more
Which will leave you
With a need to explore, more
Notice I did not say a desire, but a need
You see, one night with me, oops
I mean with a woman who you give the ability
To deeply touch your emotions
Will leave you left thirsting, searching for more
Now, I don't mean to come off too bold
But the truth must be told
Your thoughts were very well written
I just know they left someone's kitten
Hot and wet
But let's not forget
It was a very satisfying, fantastic
Passionate and fanatical night
In Hell!

So, I'm now proposing
Why settle for temporary satisfaction
When you can gain a lifetime of pleasure
Immeasurable to one night of
Hot, passionate sex
Leading to the dark gates of death and hell
Just simply seek the Lord and drink from a well
That never runs dry, a fountain of living water
Created by our Heavenly Father

Something that is totally real
Love you can truly feel
Look behind the mind of your penis
And passionate lustful desires and
Let God take control of your life
Trust in the name of Jesus Christ
And do what's right
I'm saying
Trade-in your one night of Heaven
In a lifetime of Hell
For a Heavenly life
In Heaven.

Picture Of….

Oh, the things a woman does
When she's in Love….
I anticipate receiving the thoughts of your h"art"
As you stare into the eyes of my portraits
I hope the contours of my body
Are "good enough" for you
Are you willing to wait for the proper time
That you may experience the real thing
For now, here are a few portraits
With a little something "appropriate" covering me
Oh, how I long for the opportunity
To kiss you good night, night after night
I picture waking up with you
Morning, after beautiful morning….
Only if we could share this life
I'd cherish the pleasure of being your wife.

Peter Pan

It's funny, you wished for my whole heart
You got it, I'm proud of the man in you
That won't allow your lower half
To overpower your upper half
And now I insist
That your upper half listens to your heart.
Either way, you are already my Peter Pan
You may not have known this
But from the very 1st time I laid eyes on you,
You were breathtaking
And ever since that day my mind has tried
Everything to try to erase you,
But my heart keeps screaming;
"You should let him love you!"
So, won't you take my hand and whisk me away
I would love to replace these tears of pain
And I will travel with you to "Never-land"
Where there would never, ever
Be me without you, ever again
Come get me my sweet and strong Peter Pan
And bring me home to "Happily Ever After"
"Never-hurt-again-land".

How Many???

How many thoughts
Seems like just as many as mine, no lie
But let me flip the script
And ask of you just one more time….
How many dreams do you desire to fulfill
How many goals do you want to achieve
How many wishes do you have
Uh, how many?
May I take this just a little bit deeper
How many children do you want
I'm asking numbers, specifics
Seriously,
Because if I can help you fulfill any
I'm willing
That's how I feel.

Can I

Can I confide in you, honestly; about anything?
Like I really loved listening to you Sing
And because of you I went out and
Bought Mario's CD
Yeah, you should let me, Love you.
And if I start confiding, how deep can I be
Because I'm willing
To go as deep as you will let me
Seriously; Can I?

Always/ No More Temporary Crush

I've given up on trying to forget about you
Seems my heart is more interested in getting you.
Mine always, huh?
My mind is saying, Ooh yeah
I like the sound of that, I feel the same
But my heart is saying, not good enough
Show me!
Torn between the thoughts in my own mind
Never ever wanting "US" to say good-bye
Want you in my life, like Always
It's complicated, yeah, I know
But I want to be there to watch you grow
From the young man you are today
To the successful gentleman you are becoming
Wanna be there cheering you on
Can you hear me signifying?
"Yeah, see, I told you, you could do it
I knew that you could be it
Wow, Baby, you made it."
We made it
I believe in you, now rest assured
You got me, Always!

Would You?

What if I told you
That you already purchased my heart
That technically you own it
That's right, bought and paid for
However, your merchandise and
All that comes along with it
Is much too complicated to just take
But you got to come and get it
Please proceed to receiving
And bring your receipt (your heart)
And your IDentity (yourself).
If I opened the receiving door to my heart and
All of its components, would you claim me,
Huh, Would You?

Non-Stop!

I've been thinking of you every minute
Nonstop, ever since I received your mail
You made my heartbeat stop, drop, and
Reverse— now it beats for you.
My mind was a bit confused at first
Because my heart is aiming for keeps
But now I realize, I want you, this, "US", I do!

Insecurity

Never would the words fall from my mouth
And I never imagined I could
Find them inside of me
But for the very first time in my life
I asked myself the question
"Am I good enough for Him?"

Could I be all he needs in a woman
Live up to his every expectation and more
Could I prepare his meals just the way he likes it
Fold his clothes with just the right crease

Could I always tenderly lend an ear to listen
Every time he opens his mouth,
Give him my undivided attention

Could I really treat him like the King he is
Can't believe I could wrestle with such insecurities
But before I could give you me
All of me, I'd need to know…

Could I fulfill your every wet dream,
One by one
Could I prepare any meal you desire so good,
You lick your fingers and mine

Could I quench every thirst you thought
You could have, and then some
Could I travel with you to unbelievable places
And do, impossible things
Could I sport your wedding ring indefinitely,
Forever

Could I be your only one desire,
Your only one
Could I be you and when you look in a mirror
You see me
Could we be one faithfully
Eternally
Could I rid you of your
Insecurities!

Pillow Talk

Baby oil, huh?
Only if I may rub you down too
Massage oil into every inch of your body
And while you're massaging me, please
Give extra caressing to my butt cheeks and
Inner thighs, those are my hot spots
One more secret; I'm a position freak
So, pick one, stimulate me
My emotions, my intellectual, my physical body
Send tingling sensations from my head to my feet
Okay, now I'm wet for real; I instantly get moist
At the thought of your nakedness
And right now, I'm thinking your name
Feeling your name, saying your name
You hear me moaning
Hmmmm, M****, yeah right there
I'm like Burger King, "Have it your way"
And next we lay our heads to the pillow
Talk to me, tell me your insecurities
Tell me how I make you feel
Talk to me Baby, I'm listening....

Truth or Dare

May I share with you
What was really going on that day
The previous night I went to bed
With you on my mind, as usual these days
But this time, I don't recall you leaving my mind
No, not at all; and when I woke up that morning
All I could think of was you, you, you
I had planned a "special day" for us
To work on the book
Hoping you would catch the train to me
But things didn't go as I hoped they would
I had to come to the city, at the spur of the moment
However, I couldn't shake
My urgent desire to see you again
I wanted to be face to face with you desperately
I confess, the whole truth or dare game was
Simply my excuse, and this is the truth
I'm just saying, seeing you
Was the "something" I was really up to
Nevertheless, every inch of my body
Yearned for you and my eyes told no lies
If you would have dared me to put my lips on you
I admit, it would have caught me off guard
But part of me knew that you
Wouldn't have used that game to
Take advantage of my vulnerability

At What Point/ Existence

You incidentally made me the most delicious
Glass of water ever served
You made coffee, a beverage I rarely drink
Taste delightful in my mouth
You captured my attention
For hours and hours at a time and
When your eyes shined into mine
They spoke a language I didn't even know existed

You swept me off my feet, completely
At what point did I first love you
I really don't know because the truth is
It was at a time when I sure wasn't admitting it
It was at a point in time when I thought to myself
I must be crazy because I wouldn't, couldn't stop
Thinking of you, dreaming of you, reminiscing
Missing everything about you, praying
Lord help me, what's wrong with me, save me

As far as circumstances were concerned
You were gone, you had moved on and
There was just no way you could possibly have me
On your mind this much!

And then; it happened, you responded
At a point when I needed you the most
You see, I was in a very comfortable coma
That was killing me and every time the
Death angel would come to snatch life from me
I'd lay comatose convincing myself
Life as it is right now, was good enough

I mean I wasn't dead, right?
I still had life inside of me and
Just as he literally spit in my face and
Left me to emotionally die
The power of your words knocked him down
And pierced my soul
Then I actually felt the power of the Holy Ghost
Release me from the coma!
At that point, I came back to life
And the rest is history
I was left with the existence of you and me
Together, forever, Holy Matrimony
How could this be…

The Real Me

No need to apologize, because you saw in me
What I couldn't see
You saw the *Real Woman* in me dying
Crying to be free; I had forgot she was there
I shut her up so many times
In fact, it's quite amazing
That you were able to see her
No one else in the world could see she was there
Or even dare attempt to bring her out
But you did, and so here I am-- Me, the real me
I'm waiting for you; Come get me.
I hope you know what to do with me
When I am yours, I pray you keep me close
And never shut me out, will you pray for me
Indefinitely, pure faith undoubtedly
May our love stand the tests of time
May each year get brighter, outshining the last
Together, Forever, Always— Our Motto
Divorce, Let Go— what is that?

Baby, Let Me Tell You

Baby, let me tell you
I'm willing to help you fulfill your dreams
Your mornings, your days, your afternoons
Your evenings, your nights
Your middle-of-the-nights
Just tell me and I'll do my personal best to
Make it right; You want my H"*art*", you got it
I'll ship it, as much as I can
During this difficult time
Tell me, will you do the same
Because I'm currently going through hell
But man, I love receiving your mail
And let me tell you even more
I am most definitely destined to
Rise above your nature
With you and I, the sky is the limit
Mentally, emotionally our souls are connected
And when I do come down, it will only be to
Passionately glide on your risen nature, physically
Moaning your name, the whole way down, yeah
Let me tell you, the only sensation I yearn is you
Your mind, your thoughts, your heart
Your body, the essence of your soul
How can you help me; hmmm
Give me you, ALL of you
So now you tell me
Will you help me?

All or Nothing

Now that I know you are ready
Consider me your Bride
Temporarily under construction
Our Father is preparing me for you
So, while He's currently *remodeling*
Please, tell Him how you want it.
You're right, you are way smarter
You figured it out
All or nothing
That's what it's all really about
The man who is willing to lay it all on the line
Is the man who deserves to receive it ALL
And there is no fight, no win or lose
The battle is already won
You have already begun preparation to
Give your all
And as you prepare to give of your whole self
I gladly place my fears, worries, and doubts
All on the shelf, and I walk away
Gliding down the aisle, into your arms to
Stay, FOREVER…

I Really Do

Hey you; I'm smiling again
I see you struggled with those
Three, little powerful words
That's why when I read them in a previous letter
I didn't believe that they were authentic

Because I know you
I knew that you would struggle with it
And so, I appreciate this expression in which
You kept it real, now allow me to encourage you

Never again be afraid to tell me how you feel
I'm here for you too; so please, always talk to me
Forever I'll listen to you Sing
And guess what— even though you know it
And I can't wait to really "show it"
Allow me to say it again, authentically
I really do, love you too!

Yeah

Together, forever, always
That's what's good enough for me
And you know what else I see
You at the BET Awards performing on stage
And I'm in the audience watching and enjoying
Thinking yeah, I sure do love that man…
Oh yeah, the recognition and
Success is coming, and I'm loving the fact that
You see me right there holding your hand
Because truthfully, wherever; Yeah wherever
You are is where I want to be FOREVER
Yeah!

Do You/ I Do

My heart says, yes
My mind says yes
My soul says, yes, yes
Hear the words flow from my mouth
Yes, yes, yes
I do.

I'm Down, If You're Down

First of all, let's get this straight
You're not stealing anything
You are merely claiming a love in which
You are deserving of
So, you don't need a getaway plan
And there will be no jumping out of any windows
Just seek God's perfect plan and plan to
Jump over the broom holding my hand
I know you ain't scared and I see
You're ready to go all out
But there's no need for any threats
Because as long as I have your respect
You will have me, ALL of me
And all we both stand to lose
Isn't worth having if
We don't have each other
Can I handle the pressure?
Yes, I can handle the pressure of you
Holding me, loving me, respecting me
Oh yeah, and if I fold, it will be in your arms
That you may console me, or to God
That He may do what you humanly can't
And if you fold, will you do the same
Allow me, and only me besides God
To be the one to comfort you
Let us both take hold of this love
Oh yeah, I'm down if you're down!!!

Strategically Planned

There it is, right there
Every single time we could have fell into some
Type of sexual fling, foolishly
God strategically stepped in and instead
We fell in love with each other's
Hearts, minds and soul
Something far more, deeper than the physical
And as we minister to each other in poetry
We're composing a book for the world to see
A mystery of love in its rarest form
Overcoming temptation, our battle is won
Perhaps we are strategically placed in a position to
One day soon be in each other's arms forever
Righteously; and all that I planned doesn't matter
Because it all would have went so wrong
Even though I planned on us remaining so strong
The fact is, we would have started innocently
And indeed, ended up composing passion
Physically….

An Experience

The room is perfect
Hot tub two feet from the bed
Mirrors everywhere
Let's get the water flowing, jets going
Set a romantic atmosphere
Enhance the temperature up in here
Passionately, physically, creatively
Adjust the thermostat too
Then change our clothes
Get much more comfortable
We got all night, all morning
And all afternoon
So, let us do whatever comes to mind
Intimately, sexually, freaky, kinky
You name it, and we can do it
This shall indeed be an "US" Experience—
"The Honeymoon".

Pillow Talk 2

Pillow talk, definitely
No wish to have this conversation on the phone
Rather be cozy in bed with you
Like all day long
Delightfully resting our heads on the pillow
Sharing sweet, intimate conversation
Spiritual, mental, physical sensation
Moaning and groaning and cum some more
Lay our heads back to the pillow
And I adore every curve
of your face
I trace with my eyes
Put your lips on my lips
No need for disguise
Together we guard each other's heart
Sharing true intimacy, marital blissity
I love you and you love me
May we bask in this love
For an eternity!

With You

I want you
I want to love you
I want to make love with you
I want to go to bed with you
And wake up with you
I want to cry with you
And laugh with you
I want to play with you
Pray with you; Lay with you
I want to watch movies with you
Cuddle with you
I want to talk with you
Eat with you
I want to get freaky with you
Kinky with you
Try some new things with you
I want to have a baby with you
Just be with you
Me with you
I simply want to share life with you
Forever, with you
Whenever with you
However, with you
Get creative with you
Yeah, with you…….

In My Life

I know these times are complicated
And this situation's got you frustrated
Me and you together is what we anticipated
Now we're both hurting and I hate it

I wish I knew how to ease the pain
There's got to be some way to dry all the rain
I feel like I'm going insane
Longing to be in your arms again

While laying in my bed, I feel out of place
Because every time I close my eyes, I see your face
My heartbeat keeps changing its pace
At thoughts of you vanishing without a trace

Regardless of right or wrong
This feeling is so strong
I lay awake each night and long
To hear you sing to me, just one more song

Please understand
You are so much more than my best friend
This love runs deeper than you just being my man
Feeling Husband in my life, for life, I'm just saying.

What If….

What if he's not running game
What if he loves me the same
What if he sincerely wants to marry me
What if he respects me enough to cherish me
What if he, just like me
Really believes our love is true
Pure, strong

What if he thinks I'm worth holding on to
What if he feels just as blessed as I
What if I am God's answer to his cry
What if our souls are truly connected
What if spiritually we are One
What if our union will be filled with so much
Joy and fun

What if this battle is already won
What if we are victoriously serving the Son
What if God will bless "US" according to
"OUR" faith
What if God abundantly gives us
His Mercy and Grace

What if this is our race to endure
What if in our hearts, minds and souls we are sure
What if we're literally on a pathway to the
Abundant life our Savior died for

What if we'll together minister to the lost, the
Love of Jesus Christ
What if God is taking what could've been
Wrong and making it right?

What if we ignore all your negative views
What if we keep
Our focus on the Lord
What if we'll ever-so wisely walk together on one accord
Always
What if we'll romantically be in love for the
Rest of our days
What if?

Commitment

Not a contract but a covenant
I vow to you this day
To Honor, Love and Cherish you
In every single way
I vow to submit to you accordingly
With Grace, Love and Mercy
Let US run this race
That is set before us, enduring until the end
Together, Forever, Always
May we share eternally, you and me
A true Bond and Beautiful Blessing
May we be one union
Undivided, forever United Standing tall
Let US be the greatest example of the
Greatest Love of all
Us—Committed, Inseparable; Unity and Strength
I love you from my soul, and today; I say, I do
Forever, I DO.

Is It Love or Lust?

Let us talk about sex; you were right
Your letter was unexpected but I'm cool
I absolutely love good surprises
Anytime you have anything on your mind to share
I'm listening, ready and willing to hear you

So, please always speak freely; your voice is
One of the things I love about you
I will keep it real and be quite frank with you too
I am no longer scared to love you

My guards are down; my faith is in Jesus alone and
I'm not focusing on trusting you, just loving you
This allows me to simply appreciate the beautiful
Things you say and do, and enjoy the smiles I smile
All because of you; my mind is made up to take this
All one day at a time and delight in every blessed
Moment, but make no mistake Baby, my ultimate
Goal is to please our Heavenly Father and
I'm grateful that you have decided to walk in
Faith with me; that's wonderful

My love, I really enjoyed your letter
It left me wet, but I also figured I should
Enlighten you on how I think
try to feel me….
Like poetry; Sex, to me, is an art and
Believe me, I yearn to be your personal artist
But first I must be exclusive to your heart
Right there next to God; let me explain
I do not by any means believe in the
World's system of dating and relationships

To me, exclusive does not mean boyfriend
Girlfriend, you're my man, I'm your girl
We're committed, we live together
I just ain't feeling that; this is where I am
Mentally and spiritually; My Love, it has
Nothing to do with you personally

But these are my beliefs and how I view
These things; there is no real obligation when
There is no real commitment; so, I'm saying….
Before I wrap my long legs over your shoulders
Bend over backwards, arch my back
Touch my toes, and let you lick my most delicate parts
Shouldn't I be worthy enough to own your
Last name, first; I'm not trying to sound like
I'm perfect, I just don't believe a male companion
Other than one's own husband deserves it

Even when I was young, dumb and full of cum and
Didn't quite understand, I still refused to
Go the distance, get down-right freaky without a
Sealed commitment; no, no, no

Yes, I simply believe in becoming a man's wife first
Because truthfully, and you know that I'm right
If I went the distance with every man who
Assured me I would be his wife; I'd be a whore and
Still single
See, I have already had the opportunity
To experience fabulous sex that did everything
Everything it could for my body but still it
Left me feeling empty and well, that just ain't
Good enough for me; after years of having sex
I am so ready to experience the "art" at its best

Better than either one of us has ever had before
I want to kiss and hug you and make love to
Your heart, mind, body, and soul
You should know that my tunnel is full of love
Oh yes, I have way more than just a wet hole
Too often, men bust a nut and they say their
Feelings for the lady seeped out with it
Well, that's just too darn bad, because when you
Explode inside me, I want you to release all the
Stress and pain that you carry
And when I explode I'll spit it back out all over your penis
And let it hit the covers leaving nothing but a puddle of
All the strain between us; that's right, I'm here to
Give you pure sexual healing
True love you can feel man
Get you drunk off my juices, leave your
Eyes tweaking; be the high that you needing

Dropping it because it's hot and wet is played out
And whack; I am that one to lay on my back and
Spread my legs cause you claimed it
Signed your name in it; branded your print there
Afterwards get up, and have NO shame in it
Let "US" quietly share a hot tub together
Collect our thoughts and get back to the loving
You lay back, relax and I'll rest my head on your
Chest and listen to your heartbeat, while I
Attentively hear you tell me what you dreaming,
What you thinking, give you the freedom to share
With me your deepest thoughts; I'll let you
Cry man, release all your fears, tears and every
One of your doubts; I promise I'll stay near
Until you let it all out, because I'm here for you

Let me care for you; My Love, I want you to
Taste and see that the Lord is good
You and me bonding as one in holy unity
You working me, I'm feeling you; I'm working you
You feeling me; and ain't nobody mad but
The Devil, see; I want us to make love so good
That our souls are well-pleased
You have me on my knees while you stroking it
From behind; you moaning, I'm screaming and
Both of us praising Our Father that I'm yours and
You're mine; I'm talking about making love and having a
Worship experience; but we can't do that if
We're sinning; you feel me, I love you….
Good night.

P. S., Dear My Love

My Love, trust, that if you love me and respect me
Keep me, your forever Wifey
Dwelling, in the same home, same space
Same place, yeah, same bed at night
I am the happiest woman ever
Knowing, that you won't hurt me
That from your heart, you are, forever willing
I do not care, nor am I concerned about
Worldly affairs; but I do care about who and
Where your heart calls Home

My hope is that you take good care of me
Honor, love and respect me
Be loyal and faithful, forever oh so grateful
Graceful when you look into my eyes
Gentle when you stroke between my thighs
My hope is that you tell me the truth, Always
And think before you do

Be one with me, real with yourself
Seek God in every way and all that you do
Always avoiding the fall into temptation too

My hope is that you believe in me, My Love
And know I got your back, really
You can be confident that I'm your
Ride or Die, your bite-size, down to earth
Intelligent, thoughtful, bottom chick
My Love, won't you
Walk with me and agree
Hold me up when I'm down
I'm saying, Man….

Sacrifice for me daily, planning
For me to forever submit to you
Accept and receive love, honor
and respect from me
Keep me forever saying I Do
That's right, won't you love me genuinely
Believe in US unconditionally
P.S., Dear, My Love
We are that Forever Love.

She Sizzles.......

Stay Tuned....

COMING SOON...

HE SIZZLES

www.ingramcontent.com/pod-product-compliance
Lightning Source LLC
LaVergne TN
LVHW020656100826
845148LV00012B/2517

* 9 7 8 1 7 3 6 6 2 6 2 0 7 *